ISBN 13: 978-1-964243-59-7
ISBN 10: 1-964243-59-7

Permission request(s) should be submitted to the publisher in writing at one of the addresses below:
CHEETAH® Toys & More, LLC
207 Main Street, 3rd Floor
Hartford, CT 06106 USA

Port Antonio PO
Portland, Jamaica

info@mycheetahinc.com
paulettetrowers@yahoo.com
WhatsApp: 860-781-1726
876-909-6311

MY OWN SHAPES BOOK

Circle

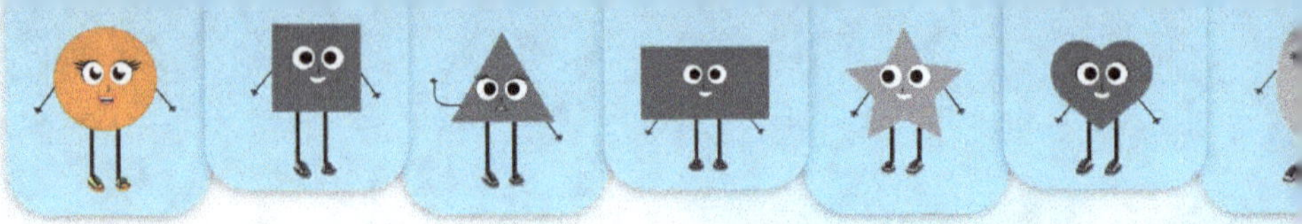

Hello. I am Mama Circle.

A circle is round.

It has no sides just like me.

Square

Look at me. I am Papa Square.

I have four sides, count with me.

1, 2, 3, 4 sides.

Triangle

Rectangle

I am Uncle Rectangle.

I have two long sides and two short sides.

Star

Look at me. I am Sister Star.

I have five points.

Touch and count my five points.

Heart

Hello, I am Grandpa Heart.

I am curvy and I have a pointy side.

Oval

Hi. I am Sister Oval. Mama circle and I are related but we are not the same.

I look like an egg.